Managing the Blended Family

Steps to Create a Stronger, Healthier Stepfamily and Succeed at Step Parenting

by Kathie M. Thomson

Published in Canada

© Copyright 2015– Kathie M. Thomson

ISBN-13: 978-1507656617
ISBN-10: 1507656610

Table of Contents

Preface 1

Chapter 1: What Are Blended Families Like Today? 3

Chapter 2: Starting Out Right 7

   Step One: You and Your Mate Begin a Discussion
about Step Parenting 8

   Step Two: Form a Plan Together 10

   Step Three: Talk to the Children about the Plan 12

   Step Four: Celebrate Coming Together 13

Chapter 3: Becoming a Loving Step Parent 15

   Ways to Act as a Loving Step Parent 15

   Developing a Family Feeling 18

Chapter 4: Communicating Effectively 23

   Common Communication Styles 24

   Communicating with Step Children 26

   The Boundary Testing Phase 28

   Communicating during Difficult Times 28

   Family Meetings 30

Chapter 5: Managing Discipline 33

   On Being Fair 35

Chapter 6: Handling Step Sibling Conflicts 37

   Step One: Stop the Argument 37

   Step Two: Get the Children to Hear Each Other 38

   Step Three: Come Up with a Solution 39

   Handling Personality Clashes 40

   Step One: Talk about Positive Qualities 40

   Step Two: Talk about Negative Qualities 40

Step Three: Lead by Example...41

Chapter 7: Coping with Ex-Spouse Bio Parents............43
  Step One: Understand that There Are No Ex-Parents
 44
  Step Two: Treat the Bio Parent with Respect.............44
  Step Three: Teach Your Stepchildren that It Is Okay to
  Love Their Other Bio Parent.......................................46
  Step Four: Control Your Jealous Feelings...................47
  Step Five: Managing Your Emotions about the Other
  Step Parent..47

Chapter 8: Keeping a Strong Relationship with Your
Mate..49
  Step One: Appreciate the Value of a Strong Marriage
 50
  Step Two: Set a Time to Talk about the Children......51
  Step Three: Have a Date Night at Least Once a Week
  without Fail...51
  Step Four: Talk about Subjects Other than Your
  Children..52
  Step Five: Make Time to Be Intimate.........................52

Chapter 9: Sharing Fun Times Together.........................55
  Appreciate Happy Moments..55
  Take in Nature Together..56
  Enjoy Fun Activities Together.....................................56
  Take Family Vacations...57
  Rent a primitive cabin...57

Conclusion...59

Preface

I want to thank you and congratulate you for choosing the book, *"Managing the Blended Family: Steps to Create a Stronger, Healthier Step Family and Succeed at Step Parenting."*

Today, more children are raised in blended families than ever before. Yet your job of being a step parent is a complex and difficult one. You have to care for your own biological children, and at the same time, you have to find a way to be a loving step parent to your new mate's children as well. You are facing a major challenge that is sure to profoundly affect your life and the lives of all the children from this moment forward.

The purpose of this book is to help you meet the challenge of step parenting by providing valuable tips on blending the family in a healthy, positive way. Once you learn new ways to think and act a step parent, this difficult task can become less stressful, more exciting and infinitely more enjoyable.

Thanks again for choosing this book, I hope you enjoy it!

Chapter 1:
What Are Blended Families
Like Today?

Are you anticipating forming a blended family in the near future? Or, have you already begun but are discovering that you need help in bringing peace and harmony to your stepfamily? You are facing one of the most important challenges of your life. Yet being a member of a blended family can be an exciting adventure for all concerned.

You can be sure that there will be rough times now and then along the way. But you can succeed in creating a happy, healthy stepfamily. All you need to do is understand the nature of the relationships, and learn and practice effective and loving ways to manage them.

First, know that you are not alone. Today, it is more common to be a member of a blended family than ever before. Here are some statistics to help you understand how normal your blended family really is:

— If you are remarried and living in the U.S., you are one of 35 million adults who are remarried after going through a divorce or becoming widowed.

— As of this writing, about one-third of all U.S. weddings create a blended family.

— Statistics show that one or both of the parents in U.S. families are stepparents in over 40% of all marriages.

— Over 95 million adults in the U.S. have some kind of step relationship, which amounts to about 42% of all U.S. adults.

Although you are one of a growing group of step parents, do not take for granted that the new family will meld well and survive – many do not. This is why it is so important to learn about how to manage your role as a stepfather or stepmother. Here are a few startling statistics to underline the importance of learning good step parenting techniques now.

- Remarrying, divorcing and remarrying again is becoming a significant trend in the U.S.

- Over 75% of people who divorce eventually remarry.

- About 33% of people who were getting a divorce in 2008 had already divorced at least once before. Researchers predict that 16% of all the people born after 1970 will follow this pattern.

- The rate of divorce for remarried couples is 34%.

- When children are exposed to this pattern of frequent transitions in and out of families, they are more likely to experience emotional and psychological problems. They also have more trouble with performance and behavior issues at school.

- The problem with failed marriages goes beyond mental health issues. Children whose parents divorce are twice as likely to have physical health issues, and live, on average, about 4 years fewer than others of their age group.

- Less than 25% of the couples that are planning to form a stepfamily ever seek parenting help before they begin living together with the children.

The good news for you, your biological children and/or your stepchildren are that you are taking steps now to avoid problems in your blended family. You want to create a great stepfamily. What an awesome gift to give to your new spouse and all the children both of you bring with you!

Chapter 2:
Starting Out Right

The ideal time to plan for the success of your blended family is before you bring the children into the step family arrangement. If you have the opportunity to plan ahead of time, do so now. When you follow this path, the transition is much less stressful for everyone concerned.

If you and your partner have already been living together in a blended family, you can still plan for a more positive family experience. As a couple, you can put the family history behind you and rethink how you manage your blended family from this moment forward.

Step One: You and Your Mate Begin a Discussion about Step Parenting

As soon as you have decided to move in and form a blended family, begin to discuss how you want to live together with all your children. The more you talk about these new relationships, the better prepared you are when you take on the roles of stepfather and stop mother.

If you are all living together already, make a date with your spouse so you can be alone together to evaluate where you are now and talk frankly about changes you want to make within the family unit. You do not have to wait for a milestone event like having a new baby or moving to a new home. Instead, have this discussion as soon as you can.

Rather than trying to force your opinions on your mate, begin by asking and answering as many questions as possible. Here is a brief list of some of the topics to discuss:

— How can you contribute to the well being of your partner's children?

— In what ways can you foster good step relationships in the family?

– What can you do to support your spouse as a stepparent?

– How can you work together to create a positive home environment?

– What can you do to show respect for your spouse as a parent and for your stepchildren as members of the family?

– How can the two of you overcome personality clashes within the family?

– What part does your co-parent want to play in building good step relationships within your blended family?

– What can you do to have a healthy and long-lasting relationship with your spouse?

– Who disciplines each of the children?

Give the question of discipline special attention. Often, the biggest stumbling block to forming a successful blended family is resentment of the stepparent. In later chapters of this book, I talk about discipline and some of the other most common and important issues you face as a stepfamily. Be sure to read through this book to get ideas before you meet for the discussion. Ask your partner if he or she is willing to read the book as well. You can have a more productive conversation if both of you start out with some common knowledge on the subject of building better step family relationships.

Try to ask your partner's opinions in a neutral way and listen actively and attentively before you contribute your own thoughts on the topic. Give your partner a chance to ask you questions or state his or her opinions as well. When you proceed this way, you create an atmosphere of mutual consideration and thoughtfulness. As you ask and answer questions, you begin a healthy give and take about the future of your blended family.

Give yourself and your partner some time to think about what you have discussed. Additional questions and concerns are likely to come up a few hours or days after your initial discussion. You can talk about these topics in depth when you come together again to discuss and formulate your plan for a successful blended family.

Step Two: Form a Plan Together

As soon as you both understand your co-parent's positions on the issues involved in blending your family, it is time to have a private planning session. Bring something to take notes on and write out your plan.

Taking the time and effort to record your decisions can be crucial to your success. Remember to let your current or future spouse look over the notes before you make any final decisions together. As you and your partner work together to formulate this plan, you begin taking on the roles of stepmother and stepfather for the first time. If you are already together, you can use this discussion to renew your commitment to the success of your blended family.

Make your plan as straightforward as you can, using concise and direct statements about how you are going to handle each issue and who is going to play the primary role in any given task. Research shows that blended families work best when each stepparent deals directly with his or her own biological children in especially difficult situations. However, there may be special circumstances where you decide that one of you should take the lead with your partner's children. For instance, a male child who has never had a positive male role model might need special attention from the stepfather. Consider each child's specific needs.

Once you have decided on the direction you want to take your step family in the future, it is time to sit the children down together to explain what you are both planning to do for them and what roles they are going to play in making your blended family a success.

Step Three: Talk to the Children about the Plan

When your plan is ready, set a date and time for your family meeting. Consult your calendars to choose a date when no one is pressed for time or occupied with something else. Select a location where you can all sit down together comfortably to talk about these life-changing plans.

Next, talk to your own biological children separately. Explain to them that you want your blended family to be healthy and happy. Let them know you have talked with your spouse about things you all can do to help. Tell them about the meeting you are going to have and encourage them to think about how they want to help your blended family on this road to success.

When you, your spouse and your children are all together, start with a positive activity. For example, you can help all of you get to know each other better. Have each child say his or her name and tell everyone one thing they want everyone to know about him or her. Your mate and stepchildren can learn new things about you and your biological children and vice versa, and you might even be surprised at what you learn about your own children.

When everyone is as comfortable as possible about talking together, tell the children what they need to know about the plans you made. Ask each of them if they have thought of any ways to help make the plan work.

When you explain your plan, there is some risk that one or more of the children will not be interested in or comfortable with the plans you made. Family transitions can be very scary and upsetting for children, so be patient with them. Explain that this is the plan, and you are going to do everything you can to help them feel comfortable as a member of your blended family.

Step Four: Celebrate Coming Together

Immediately after the meeting, do something special to celebrate your new family or your fresh start as an existing stepfamily. Choose an activity or outing that the children are likely to enjoy, in a location where none of them feels like an outsider. Usually, it is best to go somewhere neutral to both sets of children. However, if your blended family has already been living together for a while, it might be fine to do the activity in your home or yard. Whatever you do, make it a real celebration. Be actively involved in the event and show your fun side.

By ending the planning meeting with a celebration, you show the children that you are serious about creating a happy, healthy family. Enjoy this time you spend together and let the children know that there will be plenty more times to have fun together in the future.

Chapter 3:
Becoming a Loving Step Parent

One of the most common questions new stepparents ask is, "How can I feel love for a child I hardly know?" The answer is that most of the time you cannot create a feeling of love as quickly as you would like. But here is the important thing to know and remember: Love is shown in actions. Being a loving stepparent does not mean having any certain feeling. What it means is that you need to treat your stepchildren in loving ways.

Ways to Act as a Loving Step Parent

You act like a loving stepparent when you treat your mate's child with dignity and respect. Concentrate on helping the child in every appropriate way you can. As a parent, you are a teacher and mentor. You are an adult that is there to help the child find his or her way in life. You manage conflicts between your child and other, including siblings. And you gently guide the child as he or she learns right from wrong.

No child exists to make you happy or do chores you do not want to do. The lives of children are all about exploring the world and assimilating the experience and knowledge they learn from the world around them in positive and constructive ways. Your job is simply to aid in this process.

Consider the list below and think about concrete ways you can act and respond to the needs of your stepchild.

— Help your stepchild make a successful transition to a new living arrangement.

— Provide a sense of safety, security and stability.

— Show compassion for the child in everyday situations.

— Use your words and actions to build the child's positive and realistic sense of self-esteem. Remember this: praising a child when he or she does not deserve praise does not promote high self-esteem. The child will only value your praise when you focus on his or her real attributes and accomplishments.

— Encourage the child to try new activities.

- Help the child learn how to make friends and interact well in social situations.

- Never make fun of the child or criticize him or her in an unfriendly way. Avoid using sarcasm.

- Respect the child's feelings for his or her biological parents.

- Practice active listening by paying attention to what the child tells you and asking questions when you do not understand.

- Ask the child to do chores only to help him or her learn about how to be responsible and contribute to the family. Never hand out chores based on your own wants and needs.

- Help the child distinguish between reality and fantasy without being harsh or judgmental. This is particularly important with young children.

- Express disapproval of morally or legally wrong actions, but not of the child as a person.

- Protect the child's important possessions. A doll or a deck of sports cards may seem like small things to you, but the child values them just as you value your house or car. And, if they bring the items with them from their prior family home, these objects can provide comfort and security for the child in your new blended family.

— Engage with the child by planning fun and interesting activities you both can enjoy.

Do remember that you are a stepparent and not a playmate. You need to respond in a caring and helpful way when your stepchild needs assistance, guidance, acceptance and a sense of belonging. The first few months after the new family comes together can be difficult for stepparents and children alike. But you, as the adult, need to take the lead in providing support for the children and your spouse during those difficult times.

Developing a Family Feeling

Even if you do not feel close to stepchildren who have come into your life, you can help them develop a sense of belonging in your blended family. Again, focus on actions and not feelings. The good news is that the feelings often follow the actions. When you act the part of a loving stepparent, you can begin to feel the feelings that come with being a parent. Treat the child as a precious gift, and eventually the child touches your heart.

Take every opportunity to promote a sense of belonging, both for your stepchildren and your own biological children. Everyone needs to feel welcomed and valued in the family you are creating. Encourage your biological children to act in positive ways toward your stepchildren just as you do, even if they too do not feel like family yet. Here are some ways to help the children form familial bonds.

- Remind both children and stepchildren to use good manners toward their stepsiblings. Require them to say please and thank you to each other without using sarcasm.

- Have family meetings regularly and encourage everyone to participate.

- Choose one meal for all of you to share together. With young children, do it every day. Older children are often involved in extracurricular activities and spending more time with friends. If this is your situation, designate one meal that you will always share together each week

- Expect every family member to join each child in celebrating his or her birthday and other important life events. Help each child find ways to be a part of the celebration. Encourage each child to give gifts on these occasions, whether you or the child buys a gift or the child makes the gift at home or in school.

- Encourage each child to consider the feelings of the other children. Show them ways to act caring and compassionate to an upset or injured stepsibling.

— Be a kind but firm stepparent. Even if you are not the one handing out punishments, you can still take a stance that a behavior is not acceptable.

— Remember that a quiet child is not necessarily a happy, well-adjusted child. Even if the child does not complain, make it a point to talk with him or her about feelings and needs every day.

— Be fair to all the children by giving your stepchildren and biological children the attention they need.

— Be patient with your stepchildren just as you would with your own.

Lead by example. Show all the members of the blended family that living in peace and harmony is an honorable and worthwhile goal. Explain to each of them how they can benefit from doing their part to make the blended family a success. Then, be a positive role model by helping, offering kindness and support, and being a creative thinker as you find new ways to manage the problems that come your way.

The hard truth is that you are never going to be any stepchild's actual mother or father. Your role is different – it is to be a step parent who, rather than taking the place of the bio parent, instead provides a loving home for the child to live in. Yet you can become close to the child and have a very strong impact on his or her development as a healthy and loving person.

Managing a blended family is a difficult job, but when you succeed, the rewards are well worth the effort. Having a feeling of love is not the goal, although it often happens. The goal is to learn to live together in harmony.

Chapter 4:
Communicating Effectively

Experts agree that effective communication is crucial to the success of blended families. Yet good communication is not as easy as it sounds. Most families develop shortcuts for expressing thoughts and emotions. Stepchildren often feel lost and confused when their stepparent and stepsiblings say things in the language and gestures they used in their prior family.

In addition to routine communications with your children and stepchildren, you need special verbal and nonverbal techniques to get you through the tough times. Also, you can prevent problems before they start by having regular family meetings. Or, you can discuss how to solve existing problems.

You can learn to communicate what you intend to express within the context of the new stepfamily. All you need to do is consider the communication styles of everyone in the family, have patience, and think before you speak.

Common Communication Styles

Psychologists have pointed out that there are four basic styles of communication. Although these styles are not all healthy, you need to identify what style each person in the blended family is currently using. Once you have a clear understanding of how each person communicates, you can respond in a better way to help them meet individual needs.

a. Passive – People who communicate passively usually speak in a soft voice. They apologize, even when they have done nothing wrong. They use poor eye contact and limited gestures. They do not share their feelings easily. They allow others to treat them poorly and do not stand up for themselves. The biggest challenge when trying to communicate with a passive person is to find a way to help them express their thoughts and feelings.

b. Aggressive – People who have an aggressive communication style criticize, blame, interrupt and threaten. They look at you directly and intensely when they want to make a point. They use their words and gestures to control others. If someone comes to the blended family as an aggressive communicator, the temptation is to strike back. Instead, the best course of action is to stay calm, be kind and remain firm.

c. Passive-Aggressive – The passive-aggressive style is just as complex as its name suggests. The person who uses this style of communication appears to respond passively when other people speak to them. Yet behind the scenes or in subtle ways, they sabotage, use sarcasm, deny problems or mutter to themselves instead of communicating directly. When someone in your blended family uses these tactics, help him or her find better ways to express their thoughts and emotions. You cannot accept what they say as a clear expression of their thoughts and feelings, so you have to dig a little deeper to learn what they actually want to say.

d. Assertive – People who speak and behave assertively stand up for their ideas without hurting others. You do not have to guess what they are thinking and feeling. An assertive communication style is the healthiest style. If you would like to learn more about this style, you can check with your community mental health or social services for assertiveness training classes. Learn how to communicate assertively and be a role model to others in your family.

Communicating with Step Children

You have already established ways of communicating with your biological children. But those methods may fall short when you are trying to talk to your stepchildren. Your ways of talking and explaining things is new to them. If they do not know you well, they might not understand what you mean, both logically and emotionally. Here are some tips on how to communicate with your stepchildren.

— Ask clear, direct questions to eliminate ambiguity.

— Calmly state how you expect members of your blended family to behave.

— Be as specific as possible. Instead of telling the children to "Be good," tell them exactly what you mean by the phrase. (Don't climb on the cabinets, don't eat the breakfast muffins, don't play with my makeup or tools, etc.

— When a request is too broad to list every specific detail, talk about categories of behavior such as respecting other people's possessions, being kind to each other, or doing their homework.

— Always speak with an attitude of helpfulness, compassion and fairness to all.

- Express your own emotions as appropriate, but do not burden any of the children with excessive drama.

- Be an active listener. Listen to what your stepchildren tell you and ask questions if you do not understand.

- Offer suggestions when your stepchild seems at a loss for how to express something. For example, you might say, "It seems to me like you might be feeling angry." (Or use any emotion word that fits, such as sad, hurt, excited, happy, fearful, etc.). "Does that sound right?"

- Offer sincere praise when praise is due. Be fair and generous with your praise, but be realistic, too.

- Communicate as much as possible in the here and now. Avoid going back to old disagreements to prove a point. Talk about what is happening as it happens unless a past issue needs to be discussed and resolved.

- Be honest with both your children and stepchildren as much as possible. There may be times when it is best not to tell everything you know. That is okay. Instead, tell them it is something you cannot share right now.

- Use "I" messages rather than "you" messages. Own your own feelings, thoughts and values. "I feel uncomfortable with your behavior today," instead of "You are a bad child today." When you talk about your own feelings, you avoid causing the child to have low self-esteem.

The Boundary Testing Phase

As you work to create a successful blended family, be aware that most biological and stepchildren go through a phase where they are likely to test the boundaries of your good nature. This is a natural part of combining the families into one unit. Most children need to explore the situation a bit by trying out different words and behaviors. This is how they understand on an emotional level what is expected of them.

Your job during this phase is to communicate firmly, honestly and patiently. You have to be alert to the needs of each biological and stepchild so you can respond to them in appropriate ways. It is a difficult task, but when you succeed, the children will learn what you and your spouse consider to be acceptable communications within your blended family.

Communicating during Difficult Times

Hard times eventually come to all families, blended or not. However, in a blended family communications during such times can become very difficult. Some of the troublesome situations that might come up are:

- You or your spouse loses a great job
- A family member is injured in an accident
- Someone in the family contracts a life-threatening illness
- A close relative dies unexpectedly
- An unexpected expense strains the family budget
- Someone new joins the household
- One or more of your family members becomes the victim of a crime

When troubles like this occur, face them with strength. Your stepchildren, as well as your biological children, learn how to deal with problems by watching you do it. Continue to practice assertive communications skills, even when you feel hurt, lost or upset. Once again, your actions have a bigger impact than your feelings. At the same time, do not deny your feelings. Own your emotions, but explain that even if you feel that way, you can still act as a loving, caring person.

Hold onto your goal of creating a successful blended family, even when times are tough. Staying true to that special and meaningful work helps you; your spouse and the children overcome whatever adversity comes your way.

Family Meetings

Many parents only hold family meetings when they have something they want to complain about or they want to lay down the law. Broaden your definition of the family meeting, and try holding one for any of the following reasons.

- To discuss vacation plans
- To talk about a new behavior rule
- To get input from children and step children about family issues
- To encourage everyone to work together during hard times
- To teach a new interpersonal skill
- To congratulate a family member for a special achievement
- To promote family unity

In fact, it is best to have family meetings on a regular basis. Most times, once a month is adequate. But during especially stressful times including the transition period of becoming a blended family, you can have routine meetings as often as once a week. You can incorporate discussing important life events during routine family meetings, or you can devote a special meeting to that particular discussion.

Conduct the family meeting by telling everyone the topic or topics of the meeting. Then, tell the children what you and your spouse want to do about the topic. Encourage everyone to participate by stating their opinions and talking about their feelings Address everyone's needs. Then, do a relaxation exercise, listen to music together for a while, or do a fun activity together. Handle the family meeting with careful thought, giving special attention to each person. When you follow these methods, the children are more likely to look forward to participating in the next family meeting.

Chapter 5:
Managing Discipline

You probably remember a time in your life when you were disciplined unfairly. Most people have at least a few experiences with poor punishment methods even if they grew up in a happy, healthy family. Think back on a time when you were blamed for something you didn't't do or were given a harsh punishment for a minor mistake.

How did it make you feel?

What did you think of the person who gave you that unfair punishment?

Probably, you hold a lot of resentment even now if the punishment was severe or undeserved.

As a stepparent, you have to be very careful to avoid improper punishment. At the same time, you and your spouse do need to create a home with well-defined boundaries and expectations. How do you accomplish this if your stepchildren haven't learned to trust you yet?

The best way to discipline your stepchildren is to not do it at all. Instead, let you and your spouse each be responsible for disciplining his or her own biological children. Research shows that this is the most effective choice for blended families to make.

So, what do you do if your spouse is not at home when your stepchild misbehaves? When this happens, you have three main jobs.

- First, you need to diffuse the situation. Help everyone get back to a sense of normality and equilibrium as quickly as possible.

- Second, calmly state that the behavior is not acceptable in your mutual home, but do not dwell on it.

- Third, explain that your spouse will decide what should happen next because of the misbehavior. Do this without criticizing or threatening.

- Fourth, explain the situation to your spouse when he or she gets home. I will talk more about how to do this in the chapter titled "Keeping a Strong Relationship with Your Mate."

On Being Fair

You are welcoming a new child or children into your life. Since your stepchildren are not familiar with the way you handle misbehavior, they might feel that your usual corrections and punishments are unfair. After all, it is not the way their biological parents handle things.

In addition, if you bring your own biological children with you, these children are already used to the way you discipline, and any changes you make can seem equally unfair to them.

What seems most unfair to stepchildren and bio children is when punishments seem to be based on who they are rather than what they did. The fact that you are reading this book shows that you are interested in creating a happy, healthy blended family, so you probably never think you would do this. You may very well be right.

However, the child's individual perception plays a big part in how he or she receives punishments, too. If children feel you love them less than your bio kids, they will automatically feel that any punishment is unfair. They feel this disparity even more if you actually punish the two sets of children differently.

The best way to be fair is to start by discussing rules and standards with your mate before you bring the children to live together. Then, get together to discuss these issues frequently as changes occur. Make up your minds together to discipline in the ways you choose together. Then, follow through by correcting your own children as needed and allowing your spouse to correct his or her own bio kids.

In most blended families, the most effective and helpful choice for discipline issues is to each work with your own biological children. However, if you or your spouse wants to try some different way of handling discipline and correction, talk it over first. When you decide on a discipline plan together, think about how it will affect both sets of children. Then, discuss how you will foster an atmosphere where the children can respect and depend on both parents.

Chapter 6:
Handling Step Sibling Conflicts

Your stepchildren argue and fight at times. Guess what! So do your biological children. You have probably worked out how to deal with disagreements between your bio kids. As you form your blended family, you have to alter those methods so they work for all the children in the household.

Step One: Stop the Argument

Be the grownup. Rather than getting involved in the quarrel, put an end to it as quickly as possible. Tell the children that bickering is not acceptable. Then, give them a few options. For example, you can ask them if they would like to play separately, do a different activity they can both agree on, or sit down together and talk about the argument. Let them choose as they like, because all these options can put an end to the conflict. If the children choose to work it out now, try the following method to help them decide how to get along together.

Step Two: Get the Children to Hear Each Other

Sit the children down somewhere quiet. Then, tell them each that it is time to listen to the other child's viewpoint. Determine from each child's behaviors and expressions, which one is the most, upset or will have the hardest time listening.

For ease of explanation, let us say that your daughter – either your stepdaughter or bio daughter – is most upset about an argument with your step or bio son. Start with the daughter. Ask the daughter what she wants the son to know about the situation. Then, ask the son to say what the daughter wants him to hear. Finally, ask the daughter is this is what she wanted him to realize. Then, start with the son and follow the same procedure with him.

Guide the conversation as it goes back and forth. Help as necessary by offering phrases that might describe what the son or daughter want the other child to hear. Then, always say, "Does that sound right?"

Step Three: Come Up with a Solution

When each child seems to understand what the other one wants, move on to solutions. Ask both children if they can think of any ways to solve the problem they are having. If neither child has any ideas or is not willing to try thinking of any, tell them that they will have to choose one of the other options you have given them.

Sometimes, though, you might be surprised at the excellent solutions children can propose. If the son comes up with a good solution, rephrase his answer and ask if that was what he wanted to do. Then, ask the daughter to repeat the plan, and ask her if it is a good one.

If they both agree, encourage them to go do the activity the way they have agreed they want to do it. Then, when they complete the plan, ask them how it turned out. This method is very helpful in minor disputes, but it can also be beneficial in more serious conflicts.

Handling Personality Clashes

Any two people on earth can have conflicting personalities. People from different families are generally more likely to have personalities that clash with those from other families. The reasons are obvious. They each grew up with different influences in their lives, different financial means, and different attitudes. Yet as you form this new blended family, you need to find a way for even very different children to get along with each other. Here is a method to help you accomplish that goal.

Step One: Talk about Positive Qualities

Your older child comes to you saying they simply don't like their younger stepsibling. Rather than encouraging this dislike, talk to the older child about what they like about the younger child. There is bound to be something endearing about each child, and it is your job to help the child discover those positive qualities.

Step Two: Talk about Negative Qualities

Ask, "What is it you don't like about your step sibling?" If the child says, "I don't know. I just don't like her," then help him help him explore exactly what rubs him the wrong way. Then, ask him if there is any way in which that quality can be a positive thing. For example, if the child is quiet for your child's tastes, ask him if there is anything good about being quiet. Help him realize that his stepsibling is a worthwhile person even if not one your child enjoys.

Step Three: Lead by Example

Show by your actions that even people you don't particularly like can contribute to your happiness and you can contribute to theirs. Teach patience and understanding by the way you behave toward people who are just not your cup of tea. Encourage your child to treat his stepsiblings in the same ways you treat others. Praise him when he does something to help bring the family together despite differences.

Accept this fact now: not every dispute or personality clash is immediately solvable. At the same time, keep working to get these messages across in ways that do not threaten your bio or stepchildren's sense of security. The more you practice these techniques, the closer your family can become.

Chapter 7:
Coping with Ex-Spouse Bio Parents

Coping with your stepchildren's other bio parent is one of the hardest parts of being a stepparent. While some ex-spouses are kind and cooperative, all too often the opposite is true. A resentful ex-spouse can stir up trouble between you and your stepchildren, especially if the breakup between your new spouse and his or her ex-spouse ended in a bitter battle. Tension can run high as you and your spouse try to create a healthy blended family while dealing with the sometimes-negative influence of the ex-spouse.

Overcome this obstacle, and your home will be happier and healthier.

Step One: Understand that There Are No Ex-Parents

The words "mother" and "father" are extremely powerful words for children. Whether or not your stepchildren approve of their bio parents' behavior, the connection is too strong to ignore. So, what do you do when your new spouse's ex takes the children for a weekend? How do you deal with the drama he or she creates between you and your stepchildren? The very first thing you must remember is to never speak ill of any child's bio parents, either to the children or in front of them.

Step Two: Treat the Bio Parent with Respect

You may be asking now, "How can I treat someone with respect when they act so childish and hateful?" Here is the key: You may not be able to feel respect for the other bio parent, but you can still behave positively toward them. Meet anger with kindness. Respond to jealousy with acceptance. Having everyone say you are right is not important. What is important is taking responsibility for your own words and actions and actually doing the right thing.

Remember that your stepchildren watch and listen to the way you talk to their bio mother or bio father and take internal notes. They use this information in forming an opinion of you as a stepparent and of themselves as the other bio parent's children. When you say cruel things about their bio children, your stepchildren can take it very personally. To your stepchildren, it can seem like you are disapproving of and disliking them.

Accept that you cannot control how the bio parent acts and speaks. What you can do is control your own actions and words. You have to be strong. You have to believe in yourself and that you are doing the right thing to help your spouse's beloved children grow into happy and healthy adults. So, how do you show this respect? Here are a few ways to consider.

— Seek out the other bio parent's opinion on important issues.
— Always acknowledge that the bio parent still loves his or her children.
— Do not engage in any battle your spouse's ex tries to start between you and your stepchildren. Remain calm, neutral and detached from the drama.
— Stay true to yourself and your beliefs without judging the other bio parent for his or her beliefs.
— Once again, you succeed by being the grownup in the conflict.

Step Three: Teach Your Stepchildren that It Is Okay to Love Their Other Bio Parent

You can also be a wonderful influence for good by teaching your stepchildren to continue to love their other bio parent. You can help them adjust to life in your blended family without negating their feelings of conflict. Here are a few ways to help your stepchildren.

— Let your stepchildren know that their other bio parent is doing the best they can under the circumstances.

— Encourage your stepchildren to do little things for their other bio parent, such as remembering his or her birthday, offering a holiday gift, or calling the bio parent to tell him or her about important accomplishments and milestones.

— Explain to your stepchildren that, although you disagree with something the other bio parent says, you respect their parent's right to his or her own opinion.

— Ask your stepchildren how they feel about their weekend or summer visit. Offer your shoulder to cry on when times are hard, but also let them know you are happy for them if they have a good visit.

- Speak kindly of the other bio parent without condoning his or her bad actions.

Step Four: Control Your Jealous Feelings

It is natural to feel jealous when your spouse spends time discussing important matters with the person who was once his or her mate. And, it is normal to feel jealous when the other bio parent has a deeper relationship with your stepchildren than you do. But, always remember, feelings are just feelings. You do not have to let them rule your life. Instead of giving in to your emotions, be strong and do the right thing in each situation regardless of any jealousy you feel.

Step Five: Managing Your Emotions about the Other Step Parent

You do have to offer your blended family your strong and stable presence in the household. Yet it is not healthy to bury your feelings altogether. You just need to find a way to express them without hurting the others. You can do this by regularly talking to a counselor, a member of the clergy, or a trusted friend.

You can express your basic feelings to members of the household, as long as you do it without adding conflict to an already upsetting situation. You can say, "I feel very upset today." Refrain from denigrating the other bio parent. Simply state your feeling and then assure your stepchildren that they have done nothing wrong to make you feel this way.

You do not have to go into lengthy explanations or bombard your stepchildren with angry outbursts to let them know why you feel the way you do. Act with patience, caring and understanding of the conflicts your stepchildren quite naturally feel. You are an important member of the household, but you are an adult who can manage your own emotions. The children need as much help as you can offer in dealing with the situation and the mixed emotions it brings with it.

Being a good stepparent is an enormous challenge. Do not despair. With the right attitude and a good support system of friends, family and others, you can succeed in forming a cohesive blended family.

Chapter 8:
Keeping a Strong Relationship with Your Mate

One fact is certain when you are trying to form a blended family with you, your mate and all the children you each bring to the relationship. That is, that for all your efforts, you cannot form and maintain this new stepfamily without keeping the marriage together.

It is easy to get caught up with the issues surrounding bringing two different families to live together under one roof. Often the problems of the children come first and the relationship of the couple places a distant second. These issues are indeed important. After all, when the children cannot get along, it puts a strain on your couple relationship as well.

There are other barriers to a successful remarriage as well. The two of you have to work together to make the family work. If you or your spouse is not used to planning and implementing goals together with their former spouse, there can be a large learning curve as you tackle the issues of blended family life together.

And, as you are facing these challenges within your family, outside influences and circumstances also have a powerful effect on your ability and willingness to cooperate in making the family increasingly more harmonious and healthy.

Step One: Appreciate the Value of a Strong Marriage

If you find your marriage always taking the backseat to the needs of all the children, you need to reassess what is really important. Yes, the lives of the children in situations like these are difficult and require special attention. But don't forget that, a family that is headed by a loving, intimate and cooperative couple has a much higher chance of creating a stable and happy family.

Think about what you love and admire about your mate. Then, find ways to express your appreciation for these actions and personal qualities. Let your mate know how you feel about him or her, and make a promise to yourself to show your appreciation for your spouse every day.

Step Two: Set a Time to Talk about the Children

Choose a time when you and your spouse can get together each day to talk about all of your children. Select a time when you both can sit down quietly and talk seriously. Two times to avoid are right after one or both of you returns from work and right before you go to bed. Both of these times are better spent enjoying the fact that you are together.

When you do get together, discuss arguments or misbehaviors that happened during the day. Talk about how you or your spouse will manage the situation and what punishments, if any, you want to use. If any of your children have a serious problem or medical issues, this daily talk gives you a chance to talk about solutions and treatments.

Step Three: Have a Date Night at Least Once a Week without Fail

Get together with your spouse once a week, every week, to spend time alone. You do not have to spend a lot of money, either. You can make a special meal, light candles, and make it a celebration of your marriage. Have something to occupy your children during this time – at home, at a friend's house, at a community event, or at a child care center. This time is for the two of you and no one else.

Step Four: Talk about Subjects Other than Your Children

Parents have a tendency to spend a good deal of time thinking and talking about their children. After all, your children are very important to you. They need help and guidance. You have dreams for them. They are indeed an important subject to talk about.

However, you need to spend some time talking with your spouse about other subjects. Connecting on a broad range of topics helps you solidify your relationship. What is more, when your children grow up and leave home, you will still have something in common.

Step Five: Make Time to Be Intimate

In the hustle-bustle of everyday life in a blended family, intimacy between the partners can often take a back seat to the needs of the children. Your children are definitely important, and are your primary focus as you raise them to be happy, well-adjusted humans.

Do not forget, though, to spend some time being intimate with your spouse. Have sex, cuddle, share your innermost feelings, and do whatever it takes to feel that warm, loving bond. And, when you make intimacy one of your priorities, your children reap the benefit of having a loving couple at the head of the household.

Chapter 9:
Sharing Fun Times Together

Managing a blended family is serious business. The decisions you make as a parent or stepparent have profound effects on all the children for the rest of their lives. However, with all this talk about how to communicate and handle problems, one thing is still missing: you need to enjoy life and have fun together regularly.

Appreciate Happy Moments

Happy moments come to nearly every family. If you are successfully using parenting techniques to cut down on chaos and resentment, these moments happen even more often. When you feel happy, share your joy with the others. When you notice that your spouse or one of the children is smiling, show your interest. Acknowledge how happy they look, and ask them to share with everyone.

Take in Nature Together

Beautiful nature settings have a way of calming people, even in the most stressful situations. Get your blended family together and go enjoy a natural phenomenon. Go out and look at the moon or get up together to watch the sunrise. Go on a nature walk or a hike. Set out on your deck or patio together and enjoy a warm summer evening. Listen to the crickets chirp and the birds sing.

Enjoy Fun Activities Together

Plan activities to enjoy as a family. Attend a church picnic, a concert, a live show, an ethnic festival, or a sports event together. Play both active games and indoor games. Visit a national landmark or an art museum. After you try any new activity, encourage everyone to talk about whether they want to do that activity again or try something new. Ask for suggestions as you are planning. These fun outings have a way of easing tensions between siblings and stepsiblings, as long as you make sure to meet the needs of each one during the event.

Take Family Vacations

Vacations give families a chance to get away from the stresses or daily life. They can be an important way to help everyone feel closer. Get away from everything whenever you have the opportunity. Try to do it at least once a year, or more often if you can.

Vacations can be expensive if you choose luxurious hotels and restaurants and take in high-priced concerts and shows. Here are a few ideas to try if you cannot or do not want to spend the cash required for that type of vacation.

Go camping together

Rent a primitive cabin

Have a "staycation" by going to an inexpensive hotel in your hometown or a nearby larger city. Explore the attractions, park and events that are usually attended by tourists.

Have a "daycation" by spending the days doing fun activities in your community and then coming home to enjoy a yummy meal and sleep in your own beds.

Now that you have added family fun to the mix, you are well on your way to becoming that strong, healthy blended family you have dreamed of being. You are taking on an enormous challenge, but when you succeed, you can enjoy the happiness and contentment that comes from being a part of a harmoniously blended family.

Conclusion

Thank you again for reading this book!

I hope this book was able to help you to learn more about how to manage and enjoy your new blended family.

The next step is to complete your plans together with your spouse and begin putting it into action. You can have a happy, strong blended family. Believe you can, and then make it happen!

Finally, if you enjoyed this book, please take the time to share your thoughts and post a review on Amazon. It'd be greatly appreciated!

Thank you and good luck!

CALS Sidney S. McMath Branch

Customer ID: ***********5228

Items that you checked out

Title:
Managing the blended stepfamily : steps to create a stronger healthier stepfamily and succeed at step pa
ID: 37653021474443
Due: Monday, November 13, 2017

Total items: 1
Account balance: $2.00
10/30/2017 1:10 PM
Checked out: 3
Overdue: 0
Hold requests: 0
Ready for pickup: 0

Thank you!

DISCLAIMER AND/OR LEGAL NOTICES: Every effort has been made to accurately represent this book and it's potential. Results vary with every individual, and your results may or may not be different from those depicted. No promises, guarantees or warranties, whether stated or implied, have been made that you will produce any specific result from this book. Your efforts are individual and unique, and may vary from those shown. Your success depends on your efforts, background and motivation.

The material in this publication is provided for educational and informational purposes only and is not intended as medical advice. The information contained in this book should not be used to diagnose or treat any illness, metabolic disorder, disease or health problem. Always consult your physician or health care provider before beginning any nutrition or exercise program. Use of the programs, advice, and information contained in this book is at the sole choice and risk of the reader.

CPSIA information can be obtained
at www.ICGtesting.com
Printed in the USA
LVOW04s1421270416

485573LV00024B/447/P